T0107340

How to Score a Date with Your Potential Employer

How to Score
a Date
with Your Potential
EMPLOYER

Yolanda M. Owens

iUniverse, Inc.
New York   Bloomington

How to Score a Date with Your Potential Employer

Copyright © 2010 by Yolanda M. Owens

iUniverse books may be ordered through booksellers or by contacting:

iUniverse
1663 Liberty Drive
Bloomington, IN 47403
www.iuniverse.com
1-800-Authors (1-800-288-4677)

ISBN: 978-1-4502-7118-9 (sc)
ISBN: 978-1-4502-7119-6 (ebk)

Library of Congress Control Number: 2010916852

Printed in the United States of America

iUniverse rev. date: 11/09/2010

TABLE OF CONTENTS

Welcome to the Dating Game
- ♥ *The Birds and the Bees*

Living Single—Self-Awareness
- ♥ *Understanding What You Bring to the Relationship*
- ♥ *Make Yourself Uncomfortable!*
- ♥ *Establishing Your "Type"*

The Dating Profile—Résumés
- ♥ *Have Them Seeing STARS*
- ♥ *Résumé Writing Tips Checklist*
- ♥ *Action Words*
- ♥ *Sample Résumé—What to Focus On*
- ♥ *Sample Résumé—The Ideal Profile*
- ♥ *Sample Résumé—Lack of Work Experience*
- ♥ *The Truth About Cover Letters*
- ♥ *Sample Cover Letter*
- ♥ *What Not to Do —Deal Breakers*

The Bar Scene Upgrade—Networking
- ♥ *Best Places to Practice Your Pickup Lines*
- ♥ *Steps to Scoping the Territory*

Acknowledgments

I first want to thank God for His many blessings and for continuing to show me that all things are possible through Him.

To my amazing husband, James L. Owens, Jr. Although you dislike my fits of multitasking and competing with my laptop for attention, you've been my number one supporter, cheerleader, critic, advocate, and PR rep throughout this adventure. I never would have completed this project without your coaxing and making me feel as if I was the most amazing person on the planet. Thank you for always being my best friend and the absolute love of my life!

To my grandmother, Dorothy M. Malone, thank you for passing along your humor, creativity, quick wit, and straight, no-chaser candor. Those qualities and your example helped me to find my backbone in life and strive for success. Please know your spirit lives on through me, and I love you very much.

Mom, thank you for giving me my passion for helping others and for showing me that surrounding yourself with youth keeps you young. I'm happy you've watched me along my journey.

Last, to all of the fabulous students I've recruited and interacted with over the years: thank you for giving me a story to tell and for enriching my life more than you'll ever know.

Preface

Writing this book has forced me to visit my ghosts of dating past. I have to admit, I had more bad dates (blind and otherwise) than Madonna had reinventions. It was tiring! Ambushing friends to weasel information about the date du jour; carefully fashioning the perfect outfits, one-liners, and small-talk topics; wondering if there would be a second date—you know the drill. Then the job search process began: doing the employer research, finding the appropriate interview suit, learning industry buzz words, waiting to be called for a second interview—the lines between my personal and soon-to-be professional life blurred into a bipolar scene of cognitive warfare, switching gears from talking about love for long walks on the beach and foreign films to justifying my strengths, weaknesses, and potential fit for a particular company.

Then it hit me. Whether I was interacting with the boy-next-door or the business down the street, the rules of engagement in the schizophrenic dating/interviewing game were pretty similar.

You see, I have always been a relationship glutton and been fascinated with analogies, and I have used these two things throughout my career to connect with people and make advancements in my life. So when I finally got up the nerve to pen my first book, I decided to stick with the same formula and write a relationship book about finding a job. My goal was to write an informative, targeted, resourceful, and easy-to-relate-to book for young professionals (think Strunk & White meets eHarmony). And voila! This is the end result.

Now other than a few monumentally bad dates and better-forgotten job interviews, there are other experiences that qualified me to write a book on finding a job. Professionally, I've been a college recruiting specialist for the past fifteen years (aka my entire career). And I've seen just about everything you can imagine from college students (undergrad, masters, MBA, and PhD) throughout the job-seeking process. And although those stories could have filled an entire book, my purpose for writing *How to Score a Date with your Potential Employer* was to help college students avoid certain pitfalls and to provide some guidance on searching for their first professional job or internship. I took the advice I give in *How to Score a Date with your Potential Employer* from the professional experiences I've had with college students while working at Fortune 500 companies in the pharmaceutical, education, financial services, marketing, newspaper, and technology industries, as well as my own personal college-days job-hunting experiences.

So if I may take a walk down memory lane … I entered college thinking I was going to be the next public relations super-diva. It had been my aspiration since a test my eighth-grade guidance counselor gave me determined that was the ideal career for me. Well, a liberal arts curriculum kicked that notion to the curb when I found out I also liked literature, marketing, art, and working with children, and I excelled at all of them. So I changed my major four times (communications, English, marketing, and then elementary education) before I graduated—on time and with honors—and still didn't have a clue what I wanted to do. In case you're curious, I ended up with a degree in elementary education with minors in American studies and marketing. I just tell everyone I majored in indecisiveness.

Realizing the last semester of my senior year that teaching was a better form of birth control than a career choice for me, I took inventory of the skills my numerous majors had allotted me: creativity and excellent presentation and organizational skills from teaching, business acumen and sales skills from marketing courses, and excellent writing and graphics skills from English and communication classes. Armed with that, I revamped my résumé, got it critiqued at my career center, and started submitting it for every corporate business interview for which the career center would permit me to sign up. I was lucky enough to land interviews for all of the jobs to which I applied, and I ended up accepting a position as an underwriter after graduation.

Now had you asked me then what an underwriter was, I couldn't have told you. And if I had done my homework before accepting the job, I probably wouldn't have been so quick to sign the offer letter (lesson here: always know the job you'll be doing before you accept it!). Long story short, I hated being an underwriter! I was too much of a social butterfly to be chained to a desk reading loss control reports and calculating quotes. In other words, the job was a horrible fit for my personality. The good news is that I was able to rule out what I *didn't* want to do in my career. So after the six-month training period, I cut my losses and took a job in college admissions at my alma mater. This was a great fit! It combined all of my talents of writing, teaching, presenting, socializing, and marketing, and my dream of public relations! Ding! Ding! Ding! I'd hit the jackpot. And there began my career in recruiting.

I spent two years at my alma mater before taking a role as assistant director of admissions at a prominent state school in western New York (I stayed there for three years). After that I took my absolute dream job as a college relations specialist, recruiting and training college students for internships, rotational programs, and entry-level roles and have been doing that ever since at Fortune 500 companies across the industries spectrum.

Needless to say, I've been around the job-search block a few times. And trust me—my ego has had its fair share of blisters from pounding the pavement. But even at this stage in my career, I'm learning from my mistakes and experiencing dating blunders. Despite what anyone may tell you, it's not easy deciding what you're going to be when you grow up or who you'll grow old with. But once you decide who you are and who you want to be, you'll find that all the other pieces will fall into place.

That's what this book is all about: discovering who you are and packaging your self-worth in a way that will be attractive to any dating prospect. You see, most job-search books for college students tell you how to write a killer résumé and what to say to impress someone in an interview. That's great if you're auditioning for a Miss America pageant. But it misses the mark on all the preparation you need to endure to get to that killer résumé and to make sure you have something impressive to say and the experience to back it up when the interviewers call. Before you can enter the employer dating world, you need to do some self-exploration, make some mistakes, have some experiences, and ask lots of questions.

HOW TO MAKE THIS BOOK WORK FOR YOU...

I wrote *How to Score a Date with Your Potential Employer* around the subject of dating and relationships to make it relatable, transferable to other areas of your life, and hopefully fun. Again, think of this book as a Strunk & White–meets–eHarmony resource guide for your job search, something concise you can reference for quick rules and a litmus test for your compatibility with potential employers. The chapters focus on different stages needed to get you to the coveted first-date interview and provides dating and bar tips to keep you on top of the dating game. This book is not a step-by-step, all-inclusive guide to landing a job. Rather, it's the best advice I've harvested from college students and colleagues on building your confidence, making yourself seen and heard, and maturing from struggling student to polished professional. The key is discovering the resources you need to find out who you are, what you want to do, and what employer you want to do it with. Below is a list of the top five takeaways from this book and the chapters where you can find the advice associated with them:

Top 5 Dating Tips

1. Know who you are and make sure to communicate it to your potential employer. (Chapters 2 & 3)
2. Never date an employer who's offering something you're not passionate about. (Chapters 2 & 4)
3. Do your homework before each date and come prepared for any type of dating scenario. (Chapter 5)
4. Establish a network and stay connected with it. (Chapter 4)
5. Always, *always* ask questions. (Chapter 5)

Well, enough with the preface. Because I know how anxious a person can get preparing for a first date, I won't hold you any longer. Happy reading, and go score that date with your potential employer!

CHAPTER 1

WELCOME TO THE DATING GAME

THE BIRDS AND THE BEES

There are a lot of similarities between looking for a job and dating, as you put yourself out there for someone to notice you, accept you, and ultimately date/interview/hire you. There's a getting-to-know-you stage, a stage of evaluating whether you want a second date, and a stage of deciding whether you want a long-term relationship. And like dating, there are some rules of engagement. So before you're released into the world of job seeking, I'm going to exercise my parental obligation to walk you through the birds and bees of employer dating.

Patience is a virtue. Good relationships take time to develop, so enjoy the dating process. You may experience long-distance relationships, employers who take their time in calling you back or in making decisions on where they want the relationship to go. A relationship with an employer may fizzle after months of dating, or you may find yourself involved with an all-talk and no-action player. In the midst of it all, build your network, learn from your mistakes, and use the stories for small talk at your next function. The right opportunity will come, and your patience will be virtuously rewarded.

One difference between personal relationships and relationships with an employer is that the relationship is not monogamous. In other words, it's okay to date multiple employers at once before finding "the one." A matter of fact, it's encouraged! So take this one opportunity in life to spread yourself around and get to know as many employers as possible before landing your first professional relationship.

It's okay to flirt in the relationship. There's no better feeling than having multiple employers interested in you. It's a stroke to your ego and validates your marketability. So take advantage of the situation if it happens to you. The rule of thumb in the professional world is that it's best to have another job before leaving your current one. So make sure you don't burn any bridges with the other employers you "dated" during your job search. Remain in the friend zone and keep the lines of communication open, because you never know when someone from the friend zone may think of you for a new opportunity. Also, employers are notorious bird-doggers. In other words, they like going after candidates who are already taken and performing well, so remember this as you progress through your career.

You will be expected to put out. Employers will be investing a great deal of time, money, and resources to recruit you (FYI, employers do more to recruit fresh college grads than average employees), so they're expecting you to put out for them in your performance, attitude, and level of professionalism. Be prepared for the interview, arrive on time for any meetings or events planned for you, and take the time to shake hands and kiss babies by meeting with and greeting individuals during the interviews and corresponding events.

Be an ethically transparent cheater. Honesty and candor are attractive characteristics in any dating circle. Let employers know you're interviewing with other companies and exploring other opportunities. If you have other offers on the table, let them know that and your deadline dates. Employers will appreciate your honesty and do what they can to be sensitive to your other deadlines.

Never give ultimatums! This is the kiss of death in any relationship—especially in a new relationship where you have little experience. Keep in mind that you're lobbying for your first job with a plethora of college grads swimming in the same competition pool. So be careful not to beat your chest and demand a decision from an employer to adhere to your timelines and requests. Offers can be easily rescinded and given to a more gracious (and patient) candidate.

Hang with people who are already in a relationship. Contacts who are already employed are in a better position to give you access to their inner circles—their employers! Keep in contact with friends who have already graduated and may be able to refer you and keep you abreast of openings in their companies. Sorry, but your single friends are your competition. But keep them around as your support group; you can share bad date stories and learn from each other's mistakes.

You will need to kiss a lot of frogs before finding your castle. As you cruise the employer dating circle, you may find that opposites do not attract, chemistry is nonexistent, or personalities don't mesh before finding the employer that makes you exhale and gives you the warm fuzzies. Until then, be cognizant of the fact that you may get your feelings hurt and be disappointed. But the feeling of finding the right employer will make the warts you accumulated your badges of honor.

So what's the moral of the birds and bees? The long and the short of it is that relationships, whether they be personal or professional, take time, effort, and a whole lot of trial and error. It's a continuous learning experience for you, the employers you're interviewing with, and those you meet along the way. Take the time to share and reflect on your dating course, absorb and borrow advice (and anecdotes) from others, and watch yourself and your aspirations blossom. Keep in mind that opportunities stem from shared experiences. So the more experiences you have, the more aware you are of your role in those experiences, and the more you'll have to contribute to your pool of opportunities.

CHAPTER 2

LIVING SINGLE

SELF-AWARENESS

The road to finding your ideal employer can be a lonely one. However, if you're looking for a happy ending to your journey, you'll need to start the first leg of your trip flying solo. And as with many aspects of life, you need to prove yourself before moving up. Same goes with your job search. You need to know yourself before you can successfully achieve your goals. So don't be afraid to travel the road untaken or do a little self-exploration on your way to self-awareness. You'll have plenty of time for misery-loves-company further down the path. But if you're self aware, you'll be leading the misery support group instead of renewing your membership.

So what is self-awareness? You see, self-awareness, in the professional sense, is simply discovering your talents (what do you want to do?) and selecting a position/profession where you can utilize those talents in a work environment that's right for you (what's your type?). In other words, you need to marry the realization of what you're good, bad, and mediocre at with what you want, don't want, and are willing to compromise on.

Sounds like a simple enough equation, right? Well, as with any formula, it takes a lot of trial and error before you can get it right. You're going to be moving from the real world while frequenting the cutthroat world of employer dating. And with all of these worlds colliding, you'll need the wherewithal to manage the fallout and keep your composure. So in order to prepare for your transition, you need to date yourself.

You see, the whole concept of dating is taking the time to know someone better. So dating yourself is taking some alone time in order to get to know the real you—better. Dating yourself is also a surefire way to make certain you're equipped and ready to enter into a relationship. When you know the "real" you, you're less likely to cosign on opportunities that may not be right for you.

UNDERSTANDING WHAT YOU BRING TO THE RELATIONSHIP

In my experience, the biggest dating obstacle is realizing your self-worth and what you bring to the relationship. It sounds hokey, but this is where your power lies. If you know your strengths, weaknesses, talents, shortcomings, and passions, you'll be able to sell yourself and get what you want.

Picture it … It was my senior year; I'd declared my major as indecisiveness after changing it four times. My parents swore that I was going to be the oldest living senior on an AARP scholarship because I had just announced that I didn't want to work in my major—elementary education. So now that I'd decided that being a full-time teacher was a better means of birth control than a career aspiration, I had to make some serious choices: delay graduating on time by taking on another major, or work with the degree and experience I had and try to land a job in the sexy world of business. I chose the latter, revamped my résumé, and hit the interview trail. I realized that teaching had a lot of transferable skills that anyone in the business world would love to have in a person on their team.

You see, you have to be part-thespian to be a teacher. If you can keep the attention and organization of thirty eight-year-olds all day every day, then you can pretty much rule the world. So I used this to my advantage in my business interviews and sold my ability to adapt content to my audience, emphasized my communication and presentations skills, and touted my ability to capture and hold the attention of just about anyone, honed through my teaching experiences. Add to that all of the office experience I had racked up through the on-campus jobs, summer internships, and business courses I had accumulated while moving through my revolving door of majors, and companies were beating a path to my door to find out about my unconventionalism. I took lemons and branded myself as a lemonade connoisseur. But I wouldn't have been able to accomplish any of it without self-awareness or experience.

So what's the moral of this story?

❑ **Identify your marketable skills and abilities.** Given that you're a college student, your work experience is going to be limited. You'll need to draw on your other life experiences—personal, academic, professional, volunteer, and so on—to show what you're made of. Ask yourself, what do you do in your spare time? What do your friends ask your advice for? What are your hobbies? What are you good at? (Keep in mind that you don't have to like doing it.) What classes did you excel in? (They don't have to be related to your major.) You can find skills in your passions that can translate into a number of valuable assets that will make you desirable to employers and set you apart from the competition. So spend some time with yourself and ask others (e.g., professors, classmates, managers, parents, family members) what they think you're good at. You may be surprised at the hidden talents you have and how those talents can translate into a branding tool in your job search.

You'll also need to know what job-related skills you bring to the table and how to convey them in a way that makes you stand out. Are you good with people, information, data, ideas, or concepts? Are you self-sufficient, resourceful, creative, easily adaptable, energetic, and ambitious? What makes you good at these things, and how have you made improvements to the way you've done them? Which of these areas are you the strongest in (again, you don't necessarily have to like something to be good at it), and which do you enjoying doing most?

Answering these questions will help you market the true you and stand apart from the competition. It will also help you highlight your strengths when composing your dating profile (aka résumé) and demonstrate your maturity. And you know what a sexy quality maturity is in the dating game.

❑ **Get experience!** Most employers want to see some sort of work-related experience achieved during your college career because if they hire you, they'll be looking for you to put out, so to speak. Whether paid, volunteer, glamorous, or gritty, work experience shows employers you're well-rounded and able to manage your time. And it's also a good way to figure out whether you prefer managing projects or asking, "Do you want fries with that?" As I mentioned previously, after completing my student teaching, I realized that teaching wasn't what I wanted to do when I grew up. But I took the skills I learned from the experience and made my way toward the sandbox I really wanted to play in. So if your schedule permits, find a way to gain some experience in the fields you're interested in through these opportunities:

○ INTERNSHIPS	○ SUMMER JOBS
○ ON-CAMPUS JOBS	○ SELF-EMPLOYED JOBS
○ TEMP AGENCIES	○ VOLUNTEER WORK
○ SPECIAL PROJECTS	○ CAMPUS ACTIVITIES
○ EXTRA-CURRICULAR LEADERSHIP POSITIONS	○ RESEARCH PROJECTS

Whether you realize it or not, as a college student, you have a lot to offer employers. You'll find that the academic world is roughly about five years ahead of the business world in terms of technology. Employers are hungry for these skill sets but don't necessarily have the budgets to hire high-priced consultants to manage the market research, development, implementation, and integration needed. This is where you come in. Market yourself as a part-time student consultant who can manage these types of projects at a cost that's friendlier to their bottom line and with a fresh, untainted perspective. You can build a company Web site, do some benchmarking and financial modeling, write lesson plans, or conduct market research, for example. Not only will you gain valuable experience and insight into the organization, but you'll also get paid for your perspectives, be able to showcase your skills, and build some great contacts in the process.

Okay, now that I've given you all this advice on the types of experience you need to obtain, I'm sure you're asking yourself, where do I find the jobs that will supply them? Well, the following are a few Web sites to get you started.

Dating Tip

Check out potential places you'd like to live by visiting there during breaks. Try to schedule informational interviews or do some networking while you're visiting.

WHERE TO SEARCH FOR EXPERIENCE

➢ SNAGAJOB.COM (summer jobs, hourly employment)
➢ COLLEGERECRUITER.COM (internships, full-time positions)
➢ JOBS.CAMPUSGROTTO.COM (full-time positions and career tips)
➢ VAULT.COM (internships, full-time positions, salary information, employer research)

11

- ➤ **JOB-HUNT.ORG** (internships, full-time positions, salary information, employer research and career tips for college students)
- ➤ **AFTERCOLLEGE.COM** (career advice, financial tips)
- ➤ **MONSTERTRAK.COM** (entry-level positions, internships, diversity leadership opportunities)

This is not an exhaustive list by any means. This list is merely intended to be a starting point to get you moving in the right direction and begin building your job-search network. Use these sites to start and do some additional research to expand your network of connections. For more information, check out the references section at the end of the book.

MAKE YOURSELF UNCOMFORTABLE!

Learning about yourself can be exciting and intriguing. It can also be intimidating and make you a little uncomfortable. In my opinion, making yourself uncomfortable is the most important part of self-awareness. It is part of becoming more mature, responsible, and marketable. Now I'm not suggesting that you air your dirty laundry on YouTube or list your top ten embarrassing moments on your Facebook profile. What I am suggesting is that you explore and try things you normally wouldn't do to get a better sense of what you like, what you don't like, what you're willing to compromise, and what you're good, mediocre, and just plain bad at. And as a college student, you're at your prime to make yourself uncomfortable and become more self-aware. A matter of fact, you're at a four-year clinic of self-awareness with a $40,000-a-year co-pay at your current college/university. So get your student loans' worth out of the situation and make it worth your while.

If your schedule and student loans permit, take a course or elective in a subject that interests you and has absolutely nothing to do with your major or core requirements. It can be country line dancing, underwater basket weaving, music or art appreciation, cooking, wine tasting, bookkeeping—you get the picture. The key is to do something you haven't done before that will help you achieve these results:

Build your skill sets and marketable skills	Uncover a passion or talent	Connect you with people outside of your normal circle

ESTABLISHING YOUR "TYPE"

In the dating realm, your friends, family, and acquaintances have all asked you—probably ad nauseam—"So tell me what your type is." Sorry to burst your bubble, but this question will also become a staple in finding an ideal employer. Are you interested in a small or large company? Do you want to work in a big city? Are you attracted to eco-friendly companies with a strong sense of community, companies with sensitivity to work/life balance, companies that support travel and personal growth and encourage you to laugh? Because your personal happiness and financial future lie in your answer to the "type" you select, you should be honest with yourself and those posing the question.

What should you look for in your employer "type"?

❑ **Work environment**—Take some time to evaluate the type of environment you'll work best in. Remember, you will spend a good majority of your time in the workplace. So you want to make sure it's a place that will keep you engaged. Review the following list and rate how important these factors are to your contentment at work.

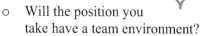

> **Dating Tip**
> *Money does not equate personal happiness (although there are those who marry for money and seem quite content with their decisions.) Don't let money be your only deciding factor.*

  o Will the position you take have a team environment?
  o Will you be an individual contributor?
  o What are the management styles?
  o Is the company culture conservative or moderate?
  o Is the dress code formal or business casual?
  o Are the employees happy with the work/life balance?
  o Are there opportunities for volunteerism?
  o Will you be able to laugh and have fun in the office?

o   What is the company's stance on diversity?

❏ **Professional Development**—Does the company offer training, classes, certifications, educational assistance for advanced degrees, mentors, or employee networks? Ask yourself how important these things are to you and then research the companies you're interested in to ensure they offer what you seek as part of their training and development or benefits package. You can usually find this information on the company's Web site under "benefits" or "professional development" sections.

❏ **Salary**—This topic should never be a deal breaker when you are considering a position. Money does not equate personal happiness (although there are those who marry for money and seem quite content with their decisions). Don't let money be your only deciding factor. I remember landing a sweet job out of college making a bucketload of money with a boatload of perks. Unfortunately, I was so hung up on the money and freebies, I failed to find out exactly what I'd be doing on the job and found out I absolutely loathed it. So I was living large on an expense account while eating Tums like it was my job, feeling depressed, and suffering from an ulcer, all at the ripe old age of twenty-three. My grandparents were in better shape than I was. So I made the decision after six months on the job to quit and take a position making ten grand less. I never looked back and was never happier! Two years later, I was making almost double what I had been making at the misery factory and have been moving up the ladder ever since. Not to sound cliché, but do what makes you happy, and the money will follow. Or if you're all about the golden goose, I suggest you make as much as you can in the short term (one to three years) and bank as much of that as you can, so that you can afford to do what really makes you happy. Everyone understands that you have to eat. But I have to admit, some of my happier times were eating ramen noodles and PB&Js as opposed to four-star swank. That's another tidbit to tuck away in the piggy bank.

❑ **Promotion potential within the company**—You have to ask yourself, is this a starter spouse or a relationship you want to build and expand on over time? Be certain to ask employers what type of career-path advancement, exposure to leadership, stretch assignments, and leadership opportunities their company offers. Keep in mind that companies base promotions on your performance and not the amount of time you spend at the company. Promotions have to be earned and are not achieved by waiting for the clock to strike midnight. So avoid asking questions such as "how long do I have to stay in this position before I can move to another department?" or "how long do I have to be with the company to become a manager?" Instead ask such questions as "How does an individual move up in your company?" or "How do you evaluate your employees and keep them challenged in their roles?" Also keep in mind that you need to be seen as well as heard in order to be recognized for your efforts. You can do the best work of anyone in your division, but unless people know who you are, you'll remain unrecognized. So find out what types of opportunities exist to interact with the movers and shakers in the company, and work on assignments outside of your area to learn about the company and expand your skills sets.

❑ **Location**—You may not think that this a big deal, but it can affect how happy you are personally with the position you take. Ask yourself, are you willing to relocate? How far are you willing to commute to and from work? How much time will it take you to get to and from work, and how expensive will it be? Do you like the community and environment you'll be living and working in? And what about social offerings? Is it important to you to live near family? What about costs of living in the suburbs as opposed to the city?

Once you've taken a personal inventory of what it is you're looking for, you'll have a better sense of yourself and the types of positions and companies you want to spend your time with. Remember, at the end of the day, you're the person accountable for your own happiness and well-being, so assess yourself now so that there will be no regrets in the future.

CHAPTER 3

THE DATING PROFILE

RÉSUMÉS

Now that you're in touch with your inner professional prowess, you need to profile it to the masses. Enter *the résumé* (aka the employer dating profile). The résumé is a one-page advertisement all about you crafted to tempt and woo would-be employers to interview you. A résumé should frame your experience in a way that whets employers' appetite, arouses their interests, and entices them to pickup the phone and get to know you better. A résumé should be intriguing, informative, and alluring, yet accurate, and it should tell a story but leave room for conversation and leave the reader wanting more. So how do you accomplish this without sounding cliché, self-absorbed, or like you're trying too hard? STARS! You've heard people say that when they met that special someone, they saw fireworks. Well, when a potential employer reads your résumé, they should see S.T.A.R.S.

imple   ruthful   ssertive   esults-driven   wagger

S.T.A.R.S.

Simple Let me tell you a recruiter's #1 pet peeve in reading résumés. It's not typos or verb tense disagreement. The thing that sets a recruiter off more than anything when reading a résumé is (drum roll please …) *fancy formatting!* That's right! We love that you're innovative and have a flair for keystrokes and text-box formatting. But at the end of the day, just keep it simple, sunshine! College recruiters can literally go through hundreds of résumés a day (my all-time high is 403 in one day) and can afford to spend only about twenty to thirty seconds on each résumé. Our eyes don't have the time or the patience to dance around the page looking for what we need. So if you want to move your résumé to the top of the stack, spend less time on font types, italics, and graphics, and focus more on the content of your experience and deliverables. Visual aesthetics don't tell employers what you're capable of. So be more graphic about what you have to offer as opposed to showing off your flair for clip art. There are more tips on how to do this effectively later in this chapter.

> *Dating Tip*
> *Keep your dating profile (resume) succinct and interesting enough to reel employers in and elusive enough to make them want to call you and ask you more.*

Truthful

For those of you who have ventured into the world of online dating, you know the frustration of reading an amazing person's profile—hot-looking, single, professional, educated, without kids, and fond of foreign films, '80s cover bands, historical fiction, and international travel. You do a little happy dance and arrange to meet the person only to learn that he or she is nothing like that fabulous profile. Now you're feeling betrayed and like your time could have been better spent alphabetizing the cans in your pantry. The same goes for the individuals reviewing your résumé. False impressions don't make the best first impressions, especially when you're trying to score a date with a desirable person or employer. Entering a new job is like coming into a new relationship—and no one wants to start a relationship on a lie. So leave the embellishments out. Employers know that as a recent grad, you won't have a truckload of professional experience. And if you try to fake the funk, your first few months will tell it and could land you in the unemployment line instead of in line for a promotion.

Also, most companies conduct background checks on prospective new hires and cross-reference dates, employers, and experiences you display on your résumé. So when composing your résumé, make it sound interesting, but keep it accurate or be prepared to be dateless or worse—in a relationship that doesn't work for anyone. Make sure you're giving accurate employment dates, school, major,

GPA (if applicable), and personal contact information on your résumé. Again, this information could be cross-referenced by a background company, and any discrepancies could cause your offer to be rescinded.

Assertive

Now when I say "assertive," I don't mean you should be a cave man, hitting a potential employer over the head and demanding they hire you. What "assertive" means with regard to your résumé is not being afraid to toot your own horn. Despite all of your home training, composing your résumé is the one time when it's okay to brag about yourself. You want to show employers that you're able to take on risks, handle challenges, lead, be innovative, be self-sufficient, and demonstrate that you have technical and interpersonal skills. So it's not the time to be modest or timid. You need to bring out the big guns (as mentioned at the beginning of this chapter) and show your professional prowess. Remember, you're competing for employers' affections, so you need to put yourself out there.

But also keep in mind that a résumé is not the medium to list every accomplishment you've made since winning your third-grade spelling bee. Your bragging needs to be strategic and focused and needs to market you and your abilities in a professional yet succinct manner. You want to keep employers intrigued by giving them enough information to get them interested and leave enough out to make them want to learn more. Hone in on the skills and abilities that will be marketable to employers and make you stand out from the competition.

And although I've used this word often in this section, keep it *professional*! Take some hints from the "Simple" section, and don't get too elaborate with your bragging rights. Tailor your résumé to fit the profile of the position you're applying to while emphasizing what it is you bring to the position and possibly other areas of the company. Also, don't be afraid to show your softer side by mentioning hobbies, volunteer work, and personal accomplishments that demonstrate leadership, sense of community, attention to detail, and time-management skills. Keep in mind that being assertive doesn't mean bulldozing. Being assertive means having enough finesse and muscle to nudge a path to your destination while keeping the respect of those you passed along the way.

R esults-Driven
At the end of the day, employers want to know what you bring to the table. And although you may not have much table experience as a college student, you do have something to contribute. So focus on your deliverables. What does that mean? For each of the positions, projects, and assignments you highlight in your résumé, also take the time to highlight what you did to improve, enhance, modify, or elevate them, and quantify the results. For example, anyone can say that he produced one hundred containers. That's pretty standard and very general. However, if you say that

you produced one hundred containers per hour with minimal defects at $.25 less per unit than standard budget, I'll give you a double take with a wink and a smile. When marketing yourself, it's not enough to just be able to do the job; you need to make the job better as a result of your abilities. So your résumé should show that you are results-driven and not just along for the ride. Show how you've taken the wheel and made for a smoother ride to successes in your accomplishments.

Swagger

Now I'm sure you've heard that nothing is sexier than confidence in the dating game.

Well, the same is true for employers looking for potential hires. Confidence is a very desirable trait. You want to make sure to show your confidence on paper as well as in person when scoping the dating territory. This means showing you put some thought and effort into your résumé before dispatching it to your desired recipient. And trust me, employers can tell who put in the effort and who was just fulfilling the obligation. Employers want to have their egos stroked and to know that you're as interested in them as they are in you. And a well-crafted, thoughtful résumé is the first step in demonstrating to them that you've got game. One of the most impressive swagger moves I've seen from a candidate was at a conference career fair. A marketing student came up to the company's information booth and saw that the representatives were overwhelmed with candidates. So she tapped one of the representatives on the arm and said, "Excuse me, I see you're a little busy right now, but I'm interested in your marketing division and wanted to leave my résumé for your consideration. Thank you for your time." And then she left. The representative was impressed by this, but more impressive was what she had attached to the résumé: she had tied a Riesen candy to the top of her résumé with a note that said, "Just wanted to provide you with a reason to review my résumé." Now that's some serious swagger. We called her that afternoon and interviewed her that very evening for a position in our marketing department. Having swagger means taking that extra step to tactfully get someone's attention and getting them to want to learn more.

Résumé Writing Tips Checklist

So now that you have stars in your eyes, let's take some steps to help you implement them into your résumé and get you noticed.

❑ **Your résumé should be only one page** unless you have significant previous/relevant experience.

❑ **Make sure your name is the first thing someone sees on your résumé.** I suggest using a 16- to 18-point font in bold to make it stand out.

❑ **Be certain to include your complete contact information.** Include your street address, state, and zip code (you'd be surprised how many people forget this!). Clearly state your campus and permanent addresses if appropriate. Also include your cell phone number and e-mail address so that a recruiter may reach you to arrange a phone screen or interview.

❑ **Use an objective in your résumé.** This helps the person reading it know in what field you're interested in working/studying. Make the objective clear, concise, and genuine. Emphasize whether you're seeking a full-time job or an internship. Make sure the objective is tailored to the specific job you're applying for (e.g., don't include an objective stating you're looking for a welding job if you're applying to a fashion magazine). If you're undecided on what you want to do, leave the objective out.

❑ **Include your Web site or blog.** If you have a Web site or blog that demonstrates examples of your work (art, Web site designs, writing samples, etc.), include that at the top of your résumé beneath your contact information.

❑ **List your degree, college/university, major, and graduation date (even if you haven't graduated).** This lets the recruiter know whether you're available for immediate hire or should be considered for their company's college recruiting program.

❑ **Include your overall GPA if it is over a 3.0.** Most companies don't look at the major GPA, so stick with the overall GPA if it's good.

❑ **Put your most significant work experience first.** Keep in mind that recruiters spend only an average of thirty seconds reading your résumé. So you want to make every word count by bulleting the most important contributions first. With that in mind, the top half of your résumé should be your best work. This is the half that will determine your résumé's potential to graduate to the top of the consideration pile or fall to the bottom of the recycling bin. You need to catch the readers' attention in the first few lines and hope they're feeling what you have to offer. If not, all you can do is pray that the company has an active recycling program and the paper sacrificed will be shredded and used to make nests for homeless birdies somewhere out there.

❑ **Use bullets when outlining your work experience.** Focus on summarizing your top three or four skills, highlights, contributions, or accomplishments for each position. This makes the résumé flow better; it's easier for you to write it this way and makes it easier for the person reading it.

❑ **When possible, use quantitative facts and deliverables to support your accomplishments.** You are competing with hundreds of others for a position, so you want to make yourself stand out. For example, there could be three hundred résumés that say that the applicant made widgets. However, if your résumé reads, "Developed a new process that increased the productivity of widget-making by 25 percent and decreased defects by 70 percent," your résumé is more likely to be noticed. Just remember to keep some balance. A résumé is not meant to detail every task you ever maneuvered throughout your work experience. Give enough detail to provide understanding, and leave enough ambiguity to pique their interest and serve as a conversation piece in the interview process.

❑ **Highlight extracurricular activities, sports, organizations, and volunteer work.** They don't call a résumé a brag sheet for nothing! Highlighting these activities shows you're well-rounded and have good time-management skills—very marketable commodities for entry-level or internship positions. It may also show a few of your hidden talents and your leadership abilities.

❏ **Mention any relevant or notable awards, recognitions, and certifications you have achieved.** The key word here is *relevant*. Being chosen for the top of the human pyramid on your high school junior varsity cheerleading squad does not make the cut in this category (yes, I have seen this listed as an accomplishment on an actual college résumé). Keep the honorable mentions academic, professional, or associated with volunteer work if appropriate (e.g., honors associations, scholarships, Big Brother, Big Sister of the year, etc). If organized sports have been a big part of your college career, feel free to list some of those accolades because they demonstrate leadership.

❏ **Be certain to include a "Computer Skills" section on your résumé.** Include all of the relevant computer applications and programs you're familiar with or proficient in, especially if these skills are noted in the job description.

❏ **Also include your fluency or proficiency in a foreign language if you applicable.** This is a marketable skill! With companies becoming more diverse and international, being multilingual could help push your résumé to the top of the stack.

❑ **If you are a foreign student, you may want to include your visa or citizenship status at the bottom of your résumé.** Many companies do not offer sponsorship for their entry-level positions and may overlook your résumé if you indicate you are from another country. If you are a citizen or permanent resident, it may be a good idea to highlight this. Again, you want to give your résumé every chance you can to move to the next level.

❑ **Spell-check and grammar-check your résumé at least twice.** Then have at least one other person you trust review it again before submitting it.

❑ **Utilize industry "buzz words" to enhance your résumé.** Review job descriptions of positions you're interested in to get a sense for these industry buzz words and scatter them throughout your résumé content. Also take the time to familiarize yourself with the buzzword meanings in case you land the interview and need to articulate what they mean.

❑ **Use action words to describe your duties and accomplishments.** This will help your résumé read and flow better. See the following chart for examples of action words. And if these don't suit your purposes, cozy up with your friendly thesaurus and expand your vocabulary (and perhaps improve your Scrabble game) in the process.

❑ **When submitting your résumé online, format it as a Word document or PDF.** These are the best formats for most online systems to upload while keeping your original résumé format.

ACTION WORDS

expedited	achieved	identified	revised	synchronized	allocated
referred	administered	installed	revamped	sorted	appraised
enabled	analyzed	instructed	restructured	classified	audited
coached	assembled	integrated	scheduled	arranged	balanced
instructed	budgeted	interviewed	sold	simplified	budgeted
wrote	built	launched	streamlined	reorganized	calculated
reconciled	collected	liaised	studied	communicated	computed
programmed	computed	managed	tested	produced	forecasted
trained	coordinated	monitored	trained	recommended	marketed
drafted	created	negotiated	updated	reviewed	projected
improved	determined	ordered	wrote	scheduled	researched
diagnosed	developed	organized	composed	generated	conceptualized
extracted	devised	performed	controlled	compiled	designed
identified	discovered	planned	investigated	specified	fashioned
summarized	evaluated	prepared	examined	screened	established
surveyed	expanded	processed	researched	validated	founded
enlisted	executed	published	presented	strengthened	assessed
edited	founded	purchased	functioned	evaluated	clarified
promoted	generated	reduced	calculated	interpreted	guided
reconciled	headed	regulated	directed	investigated	facilitated

The next section of this chapter highlights some
sample résumés to demonstrate what to do (and not
do) when composing your résumé.

Sample Résumé—What to Focus On

John Smith

41 Juniper Street • Anytown, New York 12345 • (555) 123-4567 •
person@internet.com

OBJECTIVE

> Include if you know what area you want to work

To obtain an internship that will utilize my leadership
abilities and enhance my understanding of the legal
profession.

EDUCATION

HOFSTRA UNIVERSITY, HEMPSTEAD, NEW YORK
Expected Date of Graduation: May 2007
Degree: BBA (Legal Studies in Business)
Cumulative GPA: 3.7/4.0

HONORS and AWARDS

> Always highlight RELEVANT honors and awards to show your ambition

Phi Eta Sigma Honor Society:
            Spring 2005–Present
Hofstra University Dean's List:
            December 2004–Present
New Visions Law & Government Program:
            September 2003–June 2004

EMPLOYMENT

Legal Assistant, July 2002–Present
THE DELORENZO LAW FIRM, LLP, PITTSBURGH, PA
•Extensive file maintenance
•Draft pleadings/complete discovery demands
•Assist in trial preparation

> Font too small. Never use smaller than a 10 pt. font.

32

Legislative Intern, April 2003–June 2003
SENATOR ERIC SCHNEIDERMAN'S OFFICE
ALBANY, NEW YORK
•Extensive office organization
•Performed telephone interviews with constituents

Legislative Intern, February 2004–April 2004
ASSEMBLYMAN PAUL TONKO'S OFFICE
ALBANY, NEW YORK
•Performed telephone interviews with constituents
•Observed meetings with constituents
•Prepared legislative bills for review

Intern, October 2003–December 2003
OFFICE OF ATTORNEY GENERAL
CHICAGO, ILLINOIS

Always highlight
your leadership
positions/activities

•Prepared medical timelines
•Assisted in trial preparation
•Conducted telephone interviews with potential and/or current clients

CAMPUS LEADERSHIP

Vice President of Student Activities Alumni Relations
Spring 2006–Present
•Act as intermediary between active campus community and alumni
•Chair all alumni events

Professional Events Director of Alpha Kappa Psi
Spring 2006–Present
•Create engaging professional events for fraternity members and student body
•Act as intermediary between business professionals/faculty/staff, fraternity members, and student body

President of Alpha Lambda Fall 2005
October 2005–November 2005
•Assisted in planning of professional, fund-raising, and community service events
•Chaired all general events and counseled members to fulfill their duties

33

ACTIVITIES

Alpha Kappa Psi (Fall 2004–Present); Hofstra Pre-Law Society-Phi Alpha Delta (Spring 2003–Present); College Republicans (Fall 2004–Present); Hofstra University Women's Rugby Football Club (Fall 2003–Present).

SKILLS ← Also include language skills, certifications, awards, etc.

•Microsoft Office
•WESTLAW
•LEXISNEXUS

London Synclaire

Current Address: 2164 Spruce Street, Tree, IL 24689
♦ E-mail: lsynclaire09@gmail.com ♦ Cell: 555-241-8125
Permanent Address: 81240 River Drive, Lake, FL 76543
Web site: http:/www.lsynclaire.com

OBJECTIVE
To obtain a position in Operations Management

Clear, concise objective that lets reviewer know the type of role you're interested in.

EDUCATION
University of Connecticut, Storrs, CT
Bachelor of Science in Operations Management, Expected May 2009
Cumulative GPA: 3.53

Good use of action words and varied language to describe duties in each job

PROFESSIONAL EXPERIENCE

Procurement Intern
GMS Government Contractors, *Washington, DC, May 2008–August 2008*
- Developed processes to collect pricing data for subcontracted hardware. Pricing data being used as a benchmark for future new business.
- Created visual basic macros to manage non-compete agreements in the supply chain organization. Improved efficiencies by 28%.
- Prepared agreement term documentation for procurement deals.

Corporate IT Intern
DLTM Insurance Company, *Middlebury, CT, May 2007–August 2007*
- Researched and analyzed production process dependencies. Through research was able to eliminate

34% process deficiencies and cut production costs by $37,000.
- Standardized 47 data sanitization programs.
- Designed process flows utilizing Visio to help team leaders identify future projects.

OTHER EXPERIENCE
Career Services Assistant
University of Connecticut, *Stors, CT, September 2006–Present*
- Coordinate publicity for more than 75 employment events including career fairs, employer information sessions, and speaker series. Attendance for employer information sessions increased by 15% from 2007–2008.
- Field questions and calls from clients and suggested appropriate resources.

Swim Instructor
Oakton Community Center, *Bridgeport, CT, Summers 2005–2006*
- Provided private and group swimming lessons to 35 children and young adults.
- Organized daily instructional plans.

Highlights technical, language, and professional development skills

SKILLS
Microsoft Word, Excel, PowerPoint, Access, Visio, InDesign
Conversational in Spanish
Six Sigma Yellow Belt

Demonstrates leadership, community involvement, and time management

ACTIVITIES/HONORS
President's and Dean's list all semesters
Phi Theta Kappa International Honor Society
Student Government Management Delegate
Big Brother Big Sister Volunteer
Collegiate Varsity Soccer Player
Youth Education Student Volunteer

You can still put together an impressive résumé if you lack actual work or professional experience. The key is to focus on projects, research, and academic experiences that showcase your marketable skills sets to employers.

STEPHANIE PAK

5286 Cypress Grove, Juniper Tree, WI 38912

spak429@yahoo.com (333) 555-3692

EDUCATION
Carnegie Mellon University, Pittsburgh, PA

BS Computer Engineering, May 2009

Cumulative GPA: 3.68

ACADEMIC
Design of Spa Service Web site,

Web Application Development, Spring 2009

EXPERIENCE
• Designed a Spa Service Web site using Java, JSP, HTML and MySQL

• Built three data access objects to communicate with database, and two java beans to represent records

- Managed real-time updating

UNIX, Introduction to Computer Systems, Fall 2008
- Wrote a UNIX program using C to efficiently allocate free memory space
- Designed a proxy server using C to store contents of visited Web sites

COMPUTER SKILLS
Programming Languages: C/C++, JAVA, MATLAB, HTML
Software: AutoCAD, MATLAB, Microsoft Office, Visual Studio
Operation Systems: Windows, Linux

LEADERSHIP
Teaching Assistant for Intro to Computer Systems 101 & 102
Director of Fundraising for Alpha Kappa Psi Business Fraternity
Founder of Church Youth Mentoring Program

OTHER SKILLS
Conversational in Spanish and intermediate in Japanese

ACTIVITIES
Active in intramural sports, Habitat for Humanity, and the Campus Soup Kitchen

THE TRUTH ABOUT COVER LETTERS

The truth about cover letters is … recruiters normally don't read them. We focus the bulk of our time on your résumé. As mentioned previously, recruiters can get flooded with hundreds of candidates for just one position, so time is of the essence when reviewing them. Also, in my experience, cover letters can be very deceptive; either candidates use them to suck up to whoever they think will be reading the cover letter, or they make themselves sound better than what their skills really reflect. Here's a case in point: I once got a cover letter from a candidate that was fabulous. The cover letter was well written, and it highlighted all of the managerial experience, organizational, and professional development skills that had been accumulated over the past five years. I was impressed and ready to send the candidate's résumé to the hiring manager to review. Then I flipped the cover letter over to read the candidate's résumé—the candidate worked at McDonald's managing the fry station, and everything in the cover letter was one big embellishment. So my time had been wasted, and I had to continue looking for another viable candidate. Frustrating!

A word to the wise: if you're going to submit a cover letter, stick to the facts and keep it brief. The cover letter should highlight:

☑ The position you're applying for
☑ The top two or three qualifications you bring to the position
☑ Why your skills are right for the position
☑ Your interest in speaking with someone further about the position and a telephone number where you can be reached
☑ An offering of thanks to the reader for his or her time and consideration

But on the other side of the coin, there are some instances when cover letters are useful. Cover letters can be a good litmus test of the candidate's writing ability if the position calls for strong writing skills. Most employers will specify whether they require a cover letter with the résumé submission or have it be optional. So look for this information in the job posting and act accordingly. See the cover letter example that follows to get an idea of what your cover letter should look and sound like.

STEVEN TAYLOR

17 Any Street ♦ Someplace, NY 10000 ♦ 555-444-3333 ♦
steventaylor@internet.com

March 15, 2006

Ms. Jane Smith
Potential Employer, Inc.
P.O. Box 270028
Someplace, NY 10000

Dear Ms. Smith:

I am writing to apply for the Potential Employer, Inc. Entry Level position. The position appears to fit well with my experiences and career goals.

Attached is a copy of my résumé for your review. My qualifications include

- extensive web design and programming experience through personal consultant business,
- operations management experience through several internship experiences with national contracting companies, and
- market research and data analytic skills.

I am confident that various internship and academic experiences grant me the excellent interpersonal, organizational, analytical, and administrative skills needed to be an excellent asset to Potential Employer, Inc. I am eager to advance my skill sets and believe Potential Employer, Inc. can provide me with the satisfying chance to fulfill my goals.

I would appreciate the opportunity to speak with you personally to further discuss my qualifications and learn more about this opportunity. Please feel free to contact me at 555-444-3333.

Thank you for your consideration. I look forward to speaking with you.

Regards,

Steven Taylor

Attachment

WHAT NOT TO DO...
DEAL BREAKERS

Okay, you're ready to make your big reveal in the job market. Before you release your résumé to the masses, here are a few tips to file away in the mental rolodex on *what not to do* if you don't want to be unemployed indefinitely.

❑ **Apply for jobs you're not qualified for.** There's nothing that recruiters hate more than the one candidate who applies to every position on the job board in the name of "casting a wider net." Before hitting "select all" on a company's job board, keep in mind that you don't want to annoy the people who may hold your future employment in their hands. Read the job descriptions carefully and apply for the positions that fit your skill set. This also applies to work authorization. If the job description states that candidates must be legally authorized to work in the United States indefinitely (if you are on a student visa and have OPT or CPT, this does not make you legally authorized to work in the United States indefinitely; you will need sponsorship at the end of your OPT/CPT time frame), and you know that you will require sponsorship, you should *not* apply for the position. Do your research and focus on those companies that do support sponsorship for candidates on student visas.

❑ **Make repeat calls/e-mails asking if your résumé has been received.** Recruiters can receive up to three hundred résumés for every job they have open (which can be up to twenty-five jobs). So don't take it personally if you don't receive an immediate response to your résumé submission. Also keep in mind that, with high volumes of résumés, recruiters may be able to contact only candidates they are interested in pursuing. So use the three-week rule. If you haven't heard from a company three weeks after applying for a position, give the company a brief call or e-mail to ask about your status. If you don't get a response, continue pursuing the other companies on your list and remain professional if you do receive a call later on.

❑ **Ask to schedule a phone interview after business hours.** Be respectful of the employer's time and try to be flexible in scheduling interviews. Give the person scheduling your interview at least three available times in your schedule. If you need to maneuver your schedule, ask the scheduler if you can check your calendar and call back with your availability.

❑ **Assume you're moving on to the next interview stage just because you had a phone screen.** A phone screen is merely a litmus test for the recruiter to see whether he or she would like to schedule you to speak with a hiring manager. Don't assume that a phone call guarantees you an interview. Be certain to ask the recruiter before the end of the phone call what the next steps will be and when you will know if you've advanced to the next level of the interview process. Again, remain professional. Even if you aren't a fit for the position for which you applied, you may make an impression on a recruiter for another open position.

❑ **Answer your phone when you're unavailable to talk.** Can you say voice mail? Don't answer your phone if you're in class or in a place where you can't talk. Let voice mail do its job, and call the person back when it's more convenient.

❑ **Leave a message without a return phone number.** *Always* leave a return phone number any time you return a call or leave a message. This is just common courtesy and good business practice.

❑ **Ask about salary before an offer is made.** Never initiate the salary/benefits conversation until an official offer is made or the question is asked of you first.

❑ **Fail to ask questions when asked at the end of the interview.** Never walk away from an interview without asking at least one question. You never know if a future opportunity could arise from your meeting, so always appear interested and courteous. Even if you just ask what the next steps in the process are, ask something.

❑ **Fail to send a thank you after an interview or meeting.** Always thank someone for his or her time. You never know when the person you met with could be the six degrees of separation to your big break.

CHAPTER 4

THE BAR SCENE UPGRADE

NETWORKING

A little rewind … You've learned about the birds and the bees, you've overcome your identity crisis through self-awareness, and you've penned an Oscar-worthy résumé. Now it's time to test the waters (and your pickup lines) and hit the bar scene.

You're probably thinking that because you're about to enter the "real world," the bar scene is off-limits in the name of professionalism. Not true! Upgrade to "grown-up" contact methods by changing how you invest your time. You can still cruise the bars; you just have to adapt the bar-scene circuit you're working to suit your new relationship goal of landing a hot job. Here are a few suggestions for spots you should frequent.

BEST PLACES TO PRACTICE YOUR PICKUP LINES

Six Degrees of Separation

Your best contacts could be the people you interact with every day. Begin making a list of your friends and family and then reach out to them to see whom they're connected to who may help you with your job search goals.

Alumni Networks

Check with your career center to see if they have a listing of alumni willing to assist fellow alum with their job searches. Look for alum who have occupations in your career interest areas and then contact them and request to set up an informational interview in person or via phone to discuss their career/company.

Professors

Yes, putting an apple on the professor's desk can get you an employer date. Recruiters schmooze professors to find out who the star students are.

Clerical/Support Positions

Having office skills is attractive to employers. Take a part-time job during the summer and breaks in your desired field to learn about the industry, get some exposure, and build your contacts and resume. Also, clerical staffs are the gateway to every important piece of information in an organization and will make you the "go to" person on the staff.

Career Fairs

Volunteer to coordinate career fairs instead of attending them. You'll get insider information on employers and the positions being recruited for and the chance to interact with employers *before* the fair.

Volunteer

Think of this as a résumé stimulus package. It will show employers that you're involved in your community and help you use your talents, get exposure, and gain valuable information and contacts.

Company Networking Events

Contact friends employed at companies you're interested in and offer to be their +1 at events.The exposure and contacts you'll make will be invaluable.

Professional Organizations

Become a member of as many as you can; get on their mailing lists; attend their events. Use professional networking sites such as LinkedIn to get involved and stay connected or join the company fan page on Facebook.

As any good player knows, before you hit the bar scene, you need a strategy to make the bar tab worth your efforts. The same goes for the upgraded bar scene. So here are three steps to help you put on your game face and scope the potential territory.

Steps to Scoping the Territory

Step 1	Step 2	Step 3
Set your goals	Develop your game plan	Follow up

STEP 1: SET YOUR GOALS

Before you start buying rounds, you need to ask yourself what you want to get at the end of the evening. Do you want to score twenty business cards? Be seen and heard? Find some new friends? Keep in mind that the main objectives of networking are to get exposure, make contacts, and build relationships.

Now I'm going to digress for a few moments for a trip down memory lane. Anytime I think about networking, I automatically think of prom. You see, I had this friend in high school (whom we'll call Tloula to protect the innocent). Tloula was the social butterfly, OCD planner, matchmaker friend we all knew in high school. Tloula's sole goal in high school was to network her way into scoring the best senior prom date her girlish charm could muster. So sophomore year, she put her goals to snag her ideal prom date, with room to exhale, on paper, and I've used them as my networking benchmark until this day. Here's an abridged version of Tloula's goals:

Tloula's Prom Date Goals...

1. Make sure to secure date early to keep stress to a minimum. Stress will not be allowed to ruin the experience!

2. Have backup date prospects in the wings in case original pick flakes out, moves to Tibet, or gets a better offer from Halle Berry.

3. Ideal person must be someone I can get along w/ on a daily basis, or Goal #1 will be worthless.

4. Ideal person must have a personality and be well-liked. Don't need the hottest person who may be lacking the previous two qualities and make me wish I had implemented Goal #2 sooner.

5. Ideal person has to be able to make me laugh or have a sense of humor and want to have fun. He has to make the hair, makeup, outfit, and killer shoes worth the effort at the end of it all!

6. Pick a person who's super reliable. He needs to show up when he's supposed to, pay his share, stay throughout the date, and not just have me on hand to hold the purse of the girl(s) he really wanted to be with.

So what's the moral, you ask? Well, going back to self-awareness, if you know what it is you're looking for, you'll be better equipped to identify who you need to cozy up to in order to obtain it. When networking, you need to know the type of people you want to network with, what you want from them, and what you can provide them in return in order for it to be a successful experience. Also keep in mind that the people you network with must be individuals you like because relationship-building is the name of the game. I'm not saying that everyone you encounter will need to be your potential BFF or will meet the parents, but those in your network should be people with whom you can casually get along and not feel awkward. Without this key element, your networking goals will only lead to frustration and confusion.

STEP 2: DEVELOP YOUR GAME PLAN
(AKA LITTLE BLACK BOOK)

Now that you have Tloula's benchmark goals in your arsenal, it's time to start putting together your little black book. I'm not going to lie—relationship building can be tricky and confusing and can try your patience. But don't let that deter you. Networking is a necessary evil that can benefit you well beyond landing a job. Building your network can help you find a great apartment, party planner, bank, baby sitter, mechanic, and so on. It can potentially be you personal connect-the-dots to

> **Bar Tip**
>
> The only people you can consider part of your network are those you have a relationship with.

finding whatever it is you're seeking. But remember the rules of karma, and don't be selfish. You need to give in order to get, so practice reciprocity and take a queue from the bar tips doled out here:

❏ **Mature your pickup line.** It's time to graduate beyond asking, "What's your name?" and "What's your sign?" to an approach of "Tell me something about yourself, ask me something about myself, and if we share some interests, let's continue to get to know each other better and see what develops from there." This should be the premise for your pickup line, and following are some suggestions on perfecting it.

> 1. *Use your home training.* In other words, good old-fashioned manners, common courtesy, and charm. Elevator pitches have become the new networking-advice buzz on the street and, in my opinion, are the worst advice for job seekers. Most people feel uneasy with the used car salesman approach to making acquaintances; approaching a stranger with a rehearsed, thirty-second skill set infomercial and a handshake with the objective of having said stranger assist, recommend, or hire you in some capacity seems not only far-fetched, but rude. When engaging anyone, whether a stranger on the metro or an

executive at a networking event, basic conversation skills are all you need.

2. *Stick to small talk.* If you're like me, idle conversation is the social equivalent of being forced into the dentist's chair. But it doesn't have to be that way. Arm yourself with some staple conversation pieces to lessen the anxiety for this necessary evil.

☑ Read up on current events, industry trends, and news on individuals, companies, and products that may be represented at the networking event you're attending.

> *Bar Tip*
> *If you take the time to listen and find out about those around you, people will remember you more than if you try to be the center of attention.*

☑ If you can get insider information of who will be on the guest list, Google those individuals you want to speak with to obtain insight on their professional and personal goings-on to help you build rapport. The goal is to find a common denominator with the people you want to connect with. It's hard to relate to someone with whom you have nothing in common, and your objective is to have these individuals remember you in the morning.

☑ Compose a list of questions that will get people to talk about themselves and their work or that requires an opinion or explanation. This will show that you are attentive, have good listening skills, and have a general interest in the person you're speaking with. Here are a few sample questions to consider:

☑ How has your job affected your lifestyle?

☑ If you could do things over again, would choose the same career path?

☑ Did you find that the work you're doing relates to what you learned in school?

☑ Do you think attending a public or private school plays a role in hiring decisions?

☑ How did you end up where you are now in life?

3. *Be candid and genuine.* Don't be labeled as a gold-digger on the networking circuit—you know, the person who talks to you only when she needs something and whose aura screams, "It's all about me!" any time she enters a space. All she's concerned about is making sure you know her name, occupation, and what you need to do to help her. Being candid and genuine is vital when networking. If people sense that you're being insincere, they won't want to associate with you, let alone entertain a working relationship with you. So take a tip from Tloula's playbook and make sure the individuals you're approaching are people you can get along with on a daily basis.

4. *Be interested as well as interesting.* When I was young and would get too chatty around company, my mom would give me a little nudge and whisper in my ear, "Be seen and not heard, sweetie." This was Mom's subtle way of saying, "Listen and take note of the people around you." I used to get a little upset when she would say this to me, thinking she just wanted to steal my thunder or deflect the focus I was getting to her. But as I got older, I

realized that what she was really saying was that if you take the time to listen and find out about those around you, people will remember you more than if you try to be the center of attention. This epiphany has served me well over the years and helped me maintain my relationships as opposed to being the flavor of the month. Learn to ask people questions about themselves, their work, what they're struggling with, and so on and keep in contact with them. For example, I was having a conversation at a holiday party with someone I wanted to do business with. He mentioned that he was going to be taking a trip to Puerto Rico with his family for the first time in a few weeks and was really excited about it. A few days later, I saw an article in a travel magazine on family-friendly places to explore in Puerto Rico. So I took a moment to send the article to the man with a note saying what a pleasure it was meeting him at the function and commenting that I hoped he and his family would enjoy their upcoming trip to Puerto Rico. He sent me a thank you e-mail and an invitation to meet him for lunch after he returned from his trip to Puerto Rico. The power of networking ...

5. *Establish rapport, and trust will follow.* Relationships aren't built on a business card and a smile alone. You need to find a common denominator with the person. Once you've established rapport and done some follow-up, their trust in you will follow, and a relationship will blossom, further building out your little black book.

❑ **Pinpoint where to network.** Believe it or not, you're probably already connected to the people you need to network with. That's right—use the six degrees of separation in your own personal circle to get you started. Take a few moments to make a list of your friends, relatives, neighbors, classmates, professors, parents' friends, and on and on and on. You never know who in your circle is connected to someone in the company, profession, or position in which you're interested, so put the word out among them and start setting up some informational interviews. See the next page for a little exercise to get you started.

MAKE A LIST OF YOUR INNER CIRCLE

Friends
1._____
2._____
3._____
4._____
5._____
6._____
7._____
8._____

Family
1._____
2._____
3._____
4._____
5._____
6._____
7._____
8._____

Classmates/Professors
1._____
2._____
3._____
4._____
5._____
6._____
7._____
8._____

Neighbors
1._____
2._____
3._____
4._____
5._____
6._____
7._____
8._____

Let everyone in your circle know that you're looking for opportunities, and ask if they know of individuals in their circles you can connect with. Also, do an assessment of their skills that you can use to your advantage while networking and keep a log of them for future reference.

❑ **Identify people in the group you want to meet.** Although you may not want to be the center of attention, you'll want to associate yourself with those who are.

Make nice with the movers and shakers in the groups you're networking with. These are the people who know everyone and make introductions for you. Remember that the movers and shakers like to have their egos stroked, so you definitely want to keep them in the loop and give them credit when one of their introductions materializes into something positive for you.

Also, going back to a previous tip, if you're privy to the information, *find out who's going to be attending* the networking engagement, and work your 007 magic to get some vitals on them before the event. This will help you with small talk, rapport–building, and follow-up should there be a love connection after the event has ended.

Know when to give up the ghost. You know the scenario—You begin talking with someone about how great the spinach puffs are, and the conversation goes dead. Move on and don't waste your time and energy holding up the wall with someone who's only there for the open bar and free food. Follow Tloula's Rule #4 and connect with someone with a personality, someone who's well liked. They're likely to have better connections.

❑ **Get yourself referred.** This is a little recruiter insider information. Employee referrals get pushed to the top of a recruiter's screening pile for potential jobs. So friend someone at the companies you're interested in. Employees can get anywhere from $500 to $5,000 for referrals, so it's a win-win situation.

❑ **Don't be afraid to pimp your friends.** Be a matchmaker. Cruise your little black book and find out what your friends' talents and assets are. Then use them to make some additional connections and get your friends some exposure in the process. If you have a friend who is a Web developer, and you cross paths with someone who needs a Web site built for his business, offer to make the introduction. You'll be seen as a powerful friend if you can help others through the strength of your little black book. People will remember you for this and keep you in mind when opportunities in their areas arise that can utilize your skills. And remember to follow up with your friend and the person to whom you referred him as a subtle reminder of your matchmaking prowess and to keep your name in their mental rolodexes.

STEP 3: FOLLOW UP

Now this is the most important step for achieving optimal results from the bar scene (hence the reason you've been reminded to do so throughout various portions of the book). It's a scientific fact that a person has to have at least three contacts with you before registering you in his or her brain. So follow-up is an important deposit to make in a person's memory bank. Don't make the mistake of collecting business cards, gathering information, and rubbing elbows with the right people just to let all your efforts sit idle. That's just the tip of the iceberg! You have to stay on their radar screen in order to be remembered, build rapport, establish a relationship, and ultimately earn their trust for your efforts to come to fruition. That's why people tell you it takes at least three dates to get to know a person. So here's what you need to do:

❑ **Make notes on the back of the business cards you collect.** Be certain to include the name of the event where you met the person, the date, and any interesting information you may have discussed with the person.

**XYZ Company Campus Networking event 10/3/09 @ NYU.
Recruiting for entry-level audit positions
3 children and jack-terrier named Mister, vacation to Hawaii next month, NYU alum & had Dr. Thomas for accounting**

- [ ] **Follow up with a personal note or e-mail one to three days after meeting the person.** Again, remember the three-date rule of contacts to keep your self on the radar screen. The note doesn't have to be long but should include your contact information and a reference to the information you collected on the back of the person's business card. Such an e-mail might read as follows:

Email
TO: lashton@gmail.com
FROM: idoe@yahoo.com
SUBJECT: Pleasure meeting you!

Dear Ms. Ashton,
It was a pleasure meeting you at the networking reception XYZ company hosted at NYU on Oct. 3. I greatly appreciate your taking the time to speak with me about your experience with the company as well as the opportunities in your audit division. Also, I spoke to Dr. Thomas after class yesterday. He says hello and that he would love to have you come and speak to our Audit 303 class when your schedule permits. So please feel free to contact him when you have a moment. He'd love to hear from you!

Hope you have a wonderful trip to Hawaii next week, and I look forward to keeping in contact with you.

Regards,
John Doe

❑ **Keep the person's contact information in your mailing list and send a correspondence once a quarter/periodically.** To keep the connection going, mail the person an occasional update or article, congratulations on a company accomplishment, a greeting card for a special occasion, or a simple note card to say hello or find out how the vacation or presentation, for example, went. Again, you need at least three contacts with people for them to remember you and for you to build a relationship with them. People like personal attention and having their egos stroked. So despite the saying, flattery *will* get you everywhere if you know how to use it properly and in a timely matter.

You're ready to hit the bar scene, fatten your little black book, get some exposure, meet some interesting people, and hopefully start building long-term relationships. Remember to stay genuine (nobody respects an opportunist), to practice reciprocity, to not be afraid to pimp your friends, and most importantly, to *have fun!* Jobs may come and go, but the networks you build along the way will last a lifetime. Let the bar hopping begin!

CHAPTER 5

THE BLIND DATE

INTERVIEWING

You've made it to the first date in the employment dating game—*the interview.* Congratulations! Now the real work begins. This chapter is dedicated to helping you make sure you're prepared for the interview dating experience and all the work that goes into making it successful.

RULES OF ENGAGEMENT

❑ **Cyber stalking**—You wouldn't go on a date without some vitals, and you shouldn't go into an interview without some basic information. Check out the company Web site, and Google the interviewers to get facts for rapport-building small talk. Just remember to keep it professional and tasteful. Unlike dating, with the job search you don't have to agonize about accidentally mentioning something that the interviewer hasn't told you but that you rather discovered from your stalking efforts.

❑ **The outfit**—The rules apply across the board with this one: dress to impress. Consider who you're meeting with and the position you're applying for. If you're unsure about what to wear, anonymously call the employer and ask what the company's standard dress code is for interviews. Here are a few simple standards to follow:

Dress Code for the Ladies	Dress Code for the Fellas
<ul><li>The classic business suit in a neutral color (black, navy, or dark gray)</li><li>Coordinating blouse or shirt in neutral colors</li><li>Low-heeled, conservative pumps or flats</li><li>Simple jewelry (small post or small hoop earrings, one ring, a watch, a simple necklace)</li><li>Neutral or flesh-tone pantyhose</li><li>Light, natural-looking makeup</li><li>Neatly polished or manicured nails, kept short, with neutral colored polish or French manicure</li><li>Light perfume or fragrance. No need to marinate in it, overpowering the interview with your scent or giving your</li></ul>	<ul><li>The classic business suit in a neutral color (black, navy, or dark gray)</li><li>White or coordinating long sleeve shirt</li><li>Coordinated tie</li><li>Belt</li><li>Watch (should be your only jewelry unless you wear a wedding band)</li><li>Conservative, polished shoes</li><li>Dark-colored socks (black, navy or dark gray)</li><li>Neatly cut hair and fresh shave</li><li>Clean, neatly trimmed nails</li><li>Light aftershave and cologne. As with the ladies, no need to marinate in your fragrance. Your scent should not be the lasting impression you leave behind</li></ul>

interviewer an asthma attack • Mints • Portfolio, attaché, or briefcase • Big smile • Confident attitude (not arrogance) • Firm handshake • Enthusiasm	• Mints • Portfolio, attaché, or briefcase • Big smile • Confident attitude (not arrogance) • Firm handshake • Enthusiasm

What to Leave Out of the Interview

- Gum
- Cell phone/Blackberry/Bluetooth
- iPod
- Attitude/arrogance
- Lies/embellishments about your abilities
- Cigarettes
- Sunglasses

❑ **Building Rapport**—Like dates, interviews are an opportunity for you to get more insight into the company as well as have the interviewer learn about you. You need to come across as interested as well as interesting, so use your charm (and Google-search cyber-stalking information) to ask the interviewers some questions about them and what motivates them to come to work on a daily basis. This allows you to get up close and personal without being overly obtrusive or appearing that you're trying too hard. Here are a few sample questions to get you started:

> *What has been your proudest moment at the company?*
>> *If you could change three things about your department, what would they be?*
>> *How would you describe your department's team dynamics?*
>> *What do you do to de-stress at work? (subliminal way to ask about work/life balance)*

❑ **Assessing chemistry**—At some point in the interview, your internal warning bells start chiming; the interviewer shows up late, dominates the conversation, asks nothing about you, talks incessantly about the commute to work, makes no mention about the position you're interviewing for, fails to make eye contact, and mentions eighty-five-hour work weeks and that the cafeteria has no vegetarian options. Now what do you do? Be professional, complete the interview, and thank the interviewer for his or her time. You don't want to burn any bridges. You never know when an interview encounter could turn into a six-degree-of-separation opportunity.

❑ **Setting the expectations**—You've spent some quality time with the interviewer(s), the conversation was good, it seems you were liked, and you can see yourself with this company. Will there be another interview? They said they would call, but you haven't heard anything. Did you do something wrong? Time to put on your big-person pants and take control of the situation. Establish a game plan before you leave the interview. Ask what the next steps are in the recruiting process and for an approximate timeline. If you don't hear within that timeline, follow up to inquire about your status and prepare a professional response for either outcome.

❑ **Let's just be friends**—The chemistry wasn't there, and you get the dreaded "you were great, but …" correspondence. Put on a grin (it's easier to grit your teeth that way), professionally express your disappointment, thank the interviewer for his or her time, and ask for feedback to help you with the next interview. You can also take this opportunity to recommend someone you know for the position and keep the relationship on a "friendly" basis. This will show your maturity and ability to bounce back in a difficult situation. No matter what, always end on a positive note and make sure to get the interviewer's business card for follow-up and future networking.

WHAT TYPE OF DATE WILL THIS BE?

One of the most stressful parts of the dating ritual is anticipating the type of date you're going to be on. Will the date be simple, over coffee; intimate and romantic; elaborate and posh; fun and innovative; one on one; or among friends? Employers take all of these scenarios into consideration when crafting their interview schedules (especially for new college hires) and have a bevy of situations they incorporate into wooing potential candidates.

> **Dating Tip**
>
> Remember: any contact you have with a potential employer is viewed as part of the interview process. So govern yourself accordingly

The following outlines some of the dating scenarios you may encounter during the interviewing process.

BEHAVE YOURSELF—THE BEHAVIORAL INTERVIEW

For those of you who don't believe in karma, let me introduce you to the next stage of your employment dating cycle—the behavioral interview, probably one of the most popular interviewing tactics companies employ to assess potential talent. The rationale for behavioral interviewing is based on the premise that your past behavior is a litmus test of how you will act in the future. In other words, employers are trying to discover how you acted or reacted in certain past situations to gauge whether you would perform well in a particular role or function at their company in the future. They accomplish this by asking a series of questions requiring specific examples from your professional, education, or personal experiences (yes, employers realize that the wealth of your experience portfolio will not be that expansive) that target certain competencies for college hires; the following are what employers are looking for on a behavioral interview date:

1. Leadership skills
2. Your capacity to handle stress and pressure
3. Your flexibility and ability to handle change
4. How well you take and give criticism
5. Your skills as a team player
6. Your communication and interpersonal skills

Sample Behavioral Interview Questions

1. Give me an example of an accomplishment you're extremely proud of and how you achieved it.
2. Describe a situation when you made an unpopular decision and how you handled implementing it.
3. Tell me about a time recently when your schedule was interrupted. How did you handle the situation?
4. Give me an example of a time when you had to convince a teammate to work on a project or assignment the teammate wasn't particularly thrilled about.
5. Tell me about a difficult situation you've had with a manager, coworker, or teammate and how you handled it.
6. Tell me about a time when you've had conflicting deadline dates you've had to meet and how you handled the situation.

Behavioral interviews provide a good time to assess the good, the bad, and the ugly of your skill set, social aptitude, and capability to think on your feet; it's a chance to showcase your wit, intellect, and talents or engineer your best act of humiliation. But before you put on your tap shoes, take a moment to choreograph some situations from your mental rolodex that tell a story and illustrate times when you problem-solved, led a team project, got recognition for an accomplishment, developed something innovative, thought outside the box, acted as a mediator, or were the bearer of bad news. Remember, you have a limited amount of time to tell these stories, so when storyboarding these memories, remember to make them detailed yet succinct and to *be candid;* draw from positive and appropriate professional, educational, and personal experiences; and include these points in all of your responses:

❑ **A specific situation.** The key word here is *specific.* Rather than tell the interviewer what you *would* do in a situation (a friend once described it to me as staying out of the "woulds"), a behavioral interview requires you to describe, in detail, how you handled a situation in the recent past. Feel free to reference coworkers, managers, professors, classmates, sports teammates, class project teams—you get the gist.

❑ **The steps you took to resolve or handle the situation.** The key is to highlight what *you* did in the situation. This is the one time where employers want to hear about the *I* in team and not the supporting cast. Bragging rights are permitted and encouraged in this arena. So take your opportunity to candidly and tactfully run with it to the finish line.

❑ **The end result of the situation.** Everyone loves a good ending. So stand and deliver. You should never leave your audience (in this case the interviewer) wondering, "How did it end?" Always wrap up your response by letting the interviewer know the results of your actions (good, bad, or indifferent).

Be prepared for follow-up questions requesting more specific details and asking how you would have handled the situation differently and if you were please with the outcome.

Dating Tip
When sharing your experiences, remember to make them detailed yet succinct. Be candid, and draw from positive and appropriate professional, educational, and personal experiences.

BE A TEAM PLAYER—THE PANEL INTERVIEW

Anyone who has traveled the blind-date circuit can relate to the next dating scenario. Picture it: You arrive at the blind date and walk into the unexpected times four—your date and your date's entourage. So now you're nervous, annoyed, dazed, confused, and trying to keep your composure. Sorry to take the air out of your balloon, but the panel interview is becoming common practice for employers due to time deprivation from busy interviewers and as a means to obtain multiple perspectives. No worries, though. Consider it killing several birds with one stone and turn on the charm. Never let them see you sweat!

Now that you know the situation at hand, here's how to work it to your advantage. Exhale! The panel interviewers are looking for the same things mentioned in the behavioral interview section. More than likely, the interviewers will be asking you behavioral questions (hence my reason for highlighting it first). Also bear in mind that in addition to increased perspectives from multiple interviewers, you'll also be under increased scrutiny. Be prepared to be treated like a science project and expect the interviewers to put the following under the microscope:

❑ **Your overall appearance**. All eyes and senses will be on you, from the part in your hair to the amount of fragrance you're wearing (or not), the color of your socks, and the lint on your lapel. Big Brother is watching, so bring your "A" game.

❑ **Your communication skills.** Careful attention will be paid to what you say, how you say it, and your body language while saying it. No matter what type of job you're interviewing for, interviewers will be assessing whether you have basic communication 101 skills: the ability to clearly articulate your ideas, actively listen, follow instructions, make eye contact, and appear engaged.

❑ **Your interpersonal skills.** When faced with a panel interview, chances are you'll be faced with multiple personalities. This is on purpose. Interviewers are gauging how you interact with different behaviors and temperaments under pressure. And because you may wind up working with some of the individuals you're interviewing with, they're also gauging your chemistry with the team. No pressure! Pant, pant, whew!

❑ **Your level of enthusiasm.** In my vast experience as a college recruiter, I've found that managers are more inclined to train and hire a recent grad with passion and enthusiasm than a candidate with experience who appears disinterested and unengaged. Experience may get you the interview, but you have to sell the total package, which means acting like you want to be there.

WINED AND DINED—THE LUNCH/DINNER INTERVIEW
Breaking bread has been a relationship litmus test since the day before forever. Somewhere in history,

someone came up with the idea that how an individual behaves during a meal is a good character indicator, and a behavioral interview a la mode measures a person's social graces, dining etiquette, and temperament under stress. It's a time-tested method that's been used to make treaties, decide states of nations, and determine the coveted second date. Needless to say, employers (and single people alike) are still utilizing it as part of their screening process for the perfect match. So know that if an employer extends the opportunity to relax and chat over a swanky dinner, this is another step in the interview process and not an automatic in for landing the job. You will have to sing for your supper, so to speak, so don't be lax and let your guard down.

Here's how to keep spinach out of your teeth. In other words, here's how to make the best of the lunch/dinner interview with few gaffes or a need to enter a witness protection program.

❑ **Mind your manners.** It sounds elementary, but nerves, coupled with trying to remember what fork to use, can make you lose your manners. Remember to say "please," "thank you," and "excuse me"; don't talk with your mouth full; wait for everyone's food to arrive before digging into your meal; and be kind to the wait staff. Treatment of the wait staff has been the kiss of death for many lunch/dinner interviewees. If you're rude to the wait staff, this may send up a red flag to the employer on how you would treat team members or customers with whom you may have to interact. You'll find in life, whether you're dating your potential soul mate or employer, that common courtesy goes a long way.

☐ **Make small talk.** Take the awkward time between sips of water while waiting for your food to talk with the interviewer. Put together some strategic questions before the meal that will allow you to gather information on the position and give you information to reference when selling your strengths if asked later in the interview process. Be certain to keep your listening skills attuned to what's being said. The more information you get, the easier it will be to articulate what value your skills bring to the table.

☐ **Act as the designated driver.** In other words, stay away from alcohol! If your host insists that you have a cocktail or glass of wine with him or her, remember to take it slow and sip your drink (one glass maximum).

☐ **Keep your meal order simple.** You want to minimize the opportunity for embarrassment, so stay away from ordering compromising foods such as spaghetti, chicken wings, or foods that may cause bodily functions to be indisposed. Order something simple, light, and moderately priced. Never order the most expensive item on the menu. Take the lead from the person or persons you're dining with and ask them what they'd recommend from the menu given that they're probably familiar with the restaurant. Whatever you do, don't be too overly indecisive on your meal selection. Remember, Big Brother is watching and may view you as having difficulty making decisions.

❑ **Don't feed the dog.** Starving college student status aside, don't ask for a doggy bag during the interview meal. Your focus should be on landing the job, not high-fiving yourself for scoring leftovers for the next day.

❑ **Stay in the comfort zone.** Just because you're having a casual conversation over a meal doesn't give you the license to lose your professionalism. As stated previously, your goal is to land a position, not add a restraining order to your résumé by getting too chummy with your host (who's probably a stranger) too soon. Keep questions about the person's personal life at a minimum and follow the golden rule of avoiding conversations on politics, sex, and religion.

HEEDING THE CALL –THE PHONE INTERVIEW

We've all been there. You go on vacation, spring break, or a family trip over the river and through the woods to grandma's house and meet someone you want to know better. Numbers are exchanged, anticipations rise, and the long-distance phone dating begins. The same thing happens with employers. They receive your résumé through a job board, career center, referral, or career fair and like what they see. They get contact information from your résumé and call you to schedule a phone interview to get to know you a little better. And the relationship begins.

Employers use phone interviews as a screening process to see whom they want to invite to their site for an in-person interview. They can also be used to minimize the expense of flying in a candidate from out of town. Whatever the case, be prepared to be called at any time for a phone interview, and keep the following tips in mind.

- ❑ **Bring your voice mail greeting to the adult table.** This is a major blunder I see (or hear) college students make all the time. While on the job hunt, put the theme music, slang, and silly greetings on hiatus until after you've signed your offer letter. Keep it simple: "Hi, I'm unable to take your call at this time. Please leave a message at the sound of the tone, and I'll return your call as soon as possible."

- ❑ **Check the contact information on the résumés you submit.** This is another frequent faux pas made by college students. Employers can't contact you if you don't provide them with your correct information. So make sure the information you submit is accurate and up-to-date. This includes your telephone/cell phone number and address (don't forget the street address and zip code!).

❑ **Keep everyone in the know.** Make sure that family members and roommates or housemates are aware of your job search so that they're on their best phone etiquette behavior and will take a message for you if you're out.

❑ **Know your role.** Keep a log of the positions you applied for and with what companies so that you can keep the details straight when companies call.

❑ **Be cognizant of your surroundings.** This is yet another college student fumble area. Employers realize that you're in class and expect to leave a message for you. So if you're job hunting, don't answer your phone during class or a team meeting or while fraternizing in the student union. That's why voice mail was invented! If an employer calls, and you answer at an inconvenient time, politely ask if there is another time that you can talk, and be prepared to provide the employer with several available times during business hours.

❑ **Take notes.** It's a phone interview, so you don't have to worry about anyone seeing what you're writing. Also have a copy of your résumé and a list of your accomplishments handy to discuss for easy reference.

❑ **Stay professional.** Just because you're on the phone doesn't let you off the professional hook. Treat the phone interview just as you would a face-to-face interview. Have your list of questions for the interviewer, ask for next steps in the process, and ask for the interviewer's contact information so that you can send a follow-up thank you.

COFFEE, TEA … PLEASE HIRE ME! THE OVER-COFFEE INTERVIEW

"Let's meet for coffee." In my circles, we called this the "safe" date. It gives you the chance to test the dating waters in a public domain while getting a caffeine fix and a get-out-of-jail-free card should your skim latte not mix with the other party's espresso.

Basically, the coffee interview is a scaled-down, more casual version of the dinner interview, and the same rules apply. Remain professional, sell your key attributes, be an attentive listener, and don't take up too much of the person's time. And as always, don't forget to show your gratitude for the person's time by following up with a thank you note or e-mail.

On Your Mark, Get Set ... The Speed-Dating Interview

This is a fairly new phenomenon in employer dating circles. Think of the speed dating scene in the Will Smith movie *Hitch*. You get dressed in your Sunday best and go to the company's office (dating site), where you stand around with other dating hopefuls (aka your candidate competition) and have several thirty-minute, back-to-back blind dates with individuals with whom you may potentially work. This can be a little more intimidating than the panel-date interview in that you're out in the open with your competition (more than likely they're sitting on either side of you) while you engage in your interview. Also, you will probably be on a very tight time schedule. But don't let them see you sweat! Keep your game face on and adhere to the interview advice given in this book, and you should make it to the finish line. Just remember, although this is a speed dating interview, that doesn't mean the decisions or response times will be expedited, so continue to keep your patience as a virtue.

Lights, Camera, Action! The Video Interview

Videotaping a date is not considered normal unless you're on a dating or reality show. However, in long-distance employer relationships, this has become a common practice to save time, money, and resources. With companies operating on leaner recruiting budgets and managers having less time to spend away from their offices, video interviews have become a great resource for interviewing college students. Many career centers have video conferencing technology and partner with companies unable to interview on campus in order to accommodate their schedules and maintain their recruitment relationships. So how does this work? Well, it works the same as a traditional on-campus interview. The interview will be scheduled through your career center. You'll arrive at the appointed time and go to an interview room. But instead of interviewing up close and personal with Mr. Jones, you'll be sitting in front of a camera while watching and speaking with Mr. Jones on a monitor. So although you won't be tangibly face-to-face, there are a few things you need to keep in mind.

1. **Stay calm and focused.** Don't be intimidated by the camera. Focus as though the person is in the room with you, and be relaxed. More than likely, the interviewer is just as uncomfortable with the process as you are. Show the interviewer how professional you can be in unfamiliar surroundings and score your way to a second interview.

2. **Dress to impress.** Just because this isn't an in-person interview doesn't mean that you get to dress casually. Again, treat this just like an in-person interview and dress the part by adhering to the dress tips mentioned previously.

3. **Show your enthusiasm.** Remember that you're being captured on video. So take advantage of your fifteen minutes of fame and don't curb your enthusiasm. It's easy to flat-line when you're in front of a camera, but you need to let the true you shine through and demonstrate how interested you are in the opportunity and what the person who is interviewing you has to say.

RACE TO THE FINISH—THE MARATHON INTERVIEW

Marathon interviews may take the entire day and could incorporate several of the dating scenarios mentioned previously. You could experience a behavioral interview with one individual and a panel interview with others and then meet with several others over breakfast, lunch, dinner, or coffee all in one day. Exhausting! The key is to be prepared for anything. Not all employers will give you a schedule ahead of time. And even if they do, schedules can change. Don't react as though you've been thrown off-guard. Remember, employers are looking for individuals who adapt well to change and varying situations. Roll with the punches and keep your eye on the finish line and the invaluable networking you'll accumulate along the way.

SAMPLE INTERVIEW QUESTIONS

If you get nothing else out of this section, remember this: never—and I mean never—leave an interview without asking questions. Interviews should be an opportunity for the potential employer to interview you *and* an opportunity for you to interview the potential employer. Your job with a company will hopefully be a long-term relationship. So you want to make sure it's a good fit for both parties. Here are some tips and sample questions to get you started.

- ❑ **Write down your questions and bring them with you to the interview.** This shows the interviewer that you're serious about the position you're interviewing for and took the time to prepare some thoughtful questions.

- ❑ **Channel your inner 007.** I am a firm believer that espionage is okay in the job search process. It's just another means of doing your homework on a company. After I graduated college, a friend of mine forwarded my résumé to a company without telling me, and I got called for an interview. Unfortunately, I had never heard of the company, and (I'm aging myself) Google and cyber stalking had not yet made the radar. So I put together some questions and asked my brother to call the company posing as a student conducting a class research project while I listened on the other line and took notes. My spying worked. I got candid answers straight from someone who worked in the department I was interviewing with and, subsequently, a job offer from my efforts (I didn't accept the job).

❑ **Use a little flattery.** You can also use your cyber stalking skills to Google your interviewer's background. Use the information to build some rapport during the interview. Keep it subtle, though. Your goal is to land a job, not get slapped with a restraining order. So I wouldn't advise commenting on the personal vent session you saw posted on the interviewer's Facebook page. I'm sure you wouldn't want the interviewer making conversation about the hookup you posted on your Facebook wall, either. Interviews (like dates) are more interesting when the candidate seems interested in what the interviewer has to say as opposed to only being concerned with what the job can do for the candidate. So don't be afraid to boost the interviewer's ego.

- ❏ What motivates you to come into the office every day?
- ❏ What's a typical day like in the office?
- ❏ What are the day-to-day responsibilities of this position?
- ❏ What characteristics or skills would make the person in this position successful?
- ❏ How does the company support training and development opportunities?
- ❏ What kind of assignments can I expect to work on in my first year on the job?
- ❏ What's the performance review process?
- ❏ How would you describe your management style?
- ❏ Will there be any opportunities for any decision-making in my first year?
- ❏ What characteristics would the ideal person for this position possess?
- ❏ How would you describe the office culture or team dynamics in the department?
- ❏ In your opinion, what are the biggest challenges the department will face in the next year?

INTERVIEW DEAL BREAKERS

Now that you're in the know on what you should do during an interview, here's a checklist of things you should avoid during the big event:

- ❏ **Not researching a company or reading the job description before an interview.** This shows the employer that you're not that interested in a company, or you're probably guilty of hitting the select all buttons on job boards. Either way, you'll have burned your bridges and will have to find some other way to rise from the ashes.

❑ **Not being truthful about or not self-disclosing your work-authorization status to the employer before the interview.** Again, if the job description specifies the company does not sponsor work authorization, you should not apply. However, if you're not certain about the company's policy on this subject, be certain to ask the question at the beginning of the recruitment process so that no one's time is wasted.

❑ **Not returning required paperwork on time.** If you can't return paperwork on time in the recruitment process, the employer is apt to think you won't be responsible enough to turn in assignments on time either. Perception is a powerful decision element. Don't let poor time-management ruin your job opportunity.

❑ **Arriving late.** Remember, your behavior during the recruiting process is often the employer's gauge on how you'll perform if you're hired. Give yourself plenty of time to get to your interview, and if possible, try to arrive at least fifteen minutes early. Just be there on time.

❑ **Dressing casually for an interview.** Even if you're interviewing for a position in maintenance, you should *always* dress up. Don't be afraid to ask the person scheduling you for the interview what the proper dress code is. It's better to be overdressed than underdressed for an interview. You never have a second chance to make a first impression.

- ❏ **Being arrogant/having a know-it-all attitude/behaving like you're entitled to a job.** No matter how great your credentials are, your attitude can make or break your landing that opportunity. So keep it humble and gracious and let your credentials (not your attitude) speak for you. There's a fine line between being confident in your abilities and being arrogant about what you think you deserve because of your abilities. Confidence will garner you respect; arrogance will get you shown the door.

- ❏ **Expensing car rentals, spa treatments, bar tabs, and so on if a company flies you in for an interview.** Be cognizant of the company's expense guidelines before submitting receipts for your interview expenses. Be modest and remember that everything you do is going to be a reflection of your future performance with the company if hired.

- ❏ **Falling asleep or appearing disinterested during a company presentation.** This is an automatic game-over in the job search process. This is the one time when faking it is acceptable. If you're falling asleep or finding yourself bored to tears during a presentation, perhaps you should remove this company from your list.

Interviews, like dating, are a learning experience. Some of those experiences will be good, others, not-so-much. Just remember, bad experiences make for good stories that perhaps you could use in your next behavioral interview. Likewise, unfavorable interviews can help you make good job choices, giving you the opportunity to weed out what you want and don't want and do some networking along the way.

CHAPTER 6

THE FLOWERS AND THE TREES . . .

I told you about the birds and the bees; now it's time you learned about the flowers and the trees. You've found the employer of your dreams (or at least one offering enough to pay the bills until your dream becomes reality) and moved from casual dating to a serious relationship with benefits. Now the real work begins for you to fully blossom.

Although you've graduated from your "single" status in the professional world, don't forget the lessons you learned along the way that got you there. Continue networking, conduct periodic self-awareness assessments, take yourself out of your comfort zone, and always be willing to learn from those around you. Just as you grow and evolve, so do your relationships. So take the lessons you've learned from *How to Score a Date with Your Potential Employer* and continue to revisit and recycle them throughout your career experiences. Remember, although the players may change, the relationship game will always stay the same.

Best of luck to you as you embark on your employer dating adventures. Remember to smile (as noted earlier, it's easier to grit your teeth that way) and always remain positive. The self-discovery, assertiveness, and courage you'll gain from this experience will take you far or give you enough material to write something worthwhile about it like I did and give you a sense of purpose. Whatever you do, learn from it, enjoy it, and don't forget to share along the way. You never know when your testimony may be a blessing to someone else.

DATE AND BE PROSPEROUS!

Love,

Yolanda M.Owens

R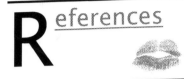eferences

Web Sites, Associations, and Organizations

The following are some additional resources to explore during the search for your employer of choice. Descriptions are taken from the organizations' Web sites. Note that inclusion in this list does not imply official endorsement by the author or publisher of the book.

Aftercollege.com
Entry-level jobs and internships for students of nursing, engineering, business, and all disciplines.
http://www.Aftercollege.com

Alpha Kappa Psi
Alpha Kappa Psi is the oldest and one of the largest professional business fraternities.
http://www.akpsi.org

The Black Collegian Online
Home page for the companion site of *The Black Collegian* magazine, featuring free career-development advice, industry profiles, and job search and résumé tips.
http://www.black-collegian.com

Campusgrotto.com
CampusGrotto.com is a national college news Web site that covers a wide range of college-related topics, including student finance, study tips, college admission, college rankings, career advice, and college life.
http://www.jobs.campusgrotto.com

CareerRookie.com
CareerRookie.com connects students and recent graduates seeking internships, part-time jobs, and entry-level jobs with the nation's top employers.
http://www.careerrookie.com

Collegegrad.com
Entry-level job site for college students and recent grads, with information on careers, résumé and cover letter writing, interviewing, jobs, salaries, and offers.
http://www.collegegrad.com

CollegeRecruiter.com
CollegeRecruiter.com is the leading job board for college students searching for employment opportunities.
http://www.collegerecruiter.com

Forte Foundation
Forté Foundation is a consortium of major corporations and top business schools that has become a powerful change agent in educating and directing talented women toward leadership roles in business.
http://www.fortefoundation.org

GradView.com
Visit GradView for information on graduate programs and career opportunities for graduate students.
http://www.gradview.com/careers

Inroads
The Inroads program was founded in 1970 with the purpose of training, counseling, and directing college-bound students toward careers in the business community.
http://www.inroads.org

Job-hunt.org

Online job search guide, listing job finders and career help on the Web. Includes tips for job hunting on the Internet, résumé writing help, and links to job sites.
http://www.Job-hunt.org

JobMonkey

Information on summer, seasonal, or year-round work in unique industries such as cruise ships, national parks, Alaskan fishing and tourism, and beach and ski resorts.
http://www.jobmonkey.com

LinkedIn

LinkedIn is a business-oriented social networking site. Founded in December 2002 and launched in May 2003, it is mainly used for professional networking.
http://www.linkedin.com

MonsterCollege

Jobs listings for college students and recent graduates. Partners with many college career centers nationwide.
http://www.monstertrak.monster.com

Monster Diversity Leadership Program
The Monster Diversity Leadership Programs (DLP) is designed to empower top college students in a dynamic, collaborative setting. These free programs offer rising sophomores, juniors, and seniors of diverse backgrounds a venue for leadership.
http://www.monsterdlp.com

NABA (National Association of Black Accountants)
Since 1969, the National Association of Black Accountants, Inc. has been the leader in expanding the influence of minority professionals in the field of accounting.
http://www.nabainc.org

New Grad Life
Visit New Grad Life today to find free help on job search, résumés, interviews, money management, and more.
http://newgradlife.blogspot.com

SnagAJob.com
Search and apply for part-time, summer, and hourly full-time jobs.
http://www.snagajob.com

Society of Hispanic Professional Engineers (SHPE)
SHPE is a leading social-technical organization whose primary function is to enhance and achieve the potential of Hispanics in engineering.
http://www.shpe.org

Society of Women Engineers (SWE)
Society of Women Engineers (SWE) is a nonprofit educational and service organization that promotes engineering as a highly desirable aspiration for women. SWE's collegiate programs provide women engineering students with training, career development services, networking, mentoring, and leadership opportunities.
http://www.swe.org

StudentJobs.Gov
Provides information on U.S. federal government job opportunities.
http://www.studentjobs.gov

SummerJobs.com
SummerJobs.com offers summer jobs and seasonal staff positions with camps, resorts, national parks, hotels, environmental organizations, and more.
http://www.summerjobs.com

Youth Venture
Youth Venture helps teams of people start new youth-led organizations.
http://www.genv.net

Vault

Insider career information, including industry and interview guides, employer profiles, employee message boards, and industry-specific job boards.
http://www.vault.com